A KID'S GUIDE TO GROWING...

SUCCULENTS

Written by
Charis Mather

KidHaven
PUBLISHING

Published in 2027 by
KidHaven Publishing, an Imprint of Greenhaven Publishing, LLC
2544 Clinton St., Buffalo, NY 14224

Written by: Charis Mather
Edited by: Beth Latham
Designed by: Rob Delph

Cataloging-in-Publication Data

Names: Mather, Charis, 1999-.
Title: Succulents / Charis Mather.
Description: Buffalo, NY : KidHaven Publishing, 2027. | Series: A kid's guide to growing... | Includes glossary and index.
Identifiers: ISBN 9781534569928 (pbk.) | ISBN 9781534569935 (library bound) | ISBN 9781534569942 (ebook)
Subjects: LCSH: Succulent plants--Juvenile literature.
Classification: LCC SB438.M38 2027 | DDC 635.9525--dc23

Printed in China

CPSIA compliance information: Batch #QS27KH: For further information contact Greenhaven Publishing LLC at 1-844-317-7404.

Please visit our website, www.greenhavenpublishing.com.
For a free color catalog of all our high-quality books, call toll free 1-844-317-7404 or fax 1-844-317-7405.

Find us on

Image Credits

Images courtesy of Shutterstock.com, unless otherwise stated.
Cover and recurring – eliyashevskiy, Torontotokio, Erika Kirkpatrick, Scisetti Alfio, Taweesak Sriwannawit, Roman Samborskyi. 2–3 – myboys.me, Linda Bestwick, hena cher. 4–5 – Golubovy, Stock_Koom. 6–7 – Christina Siow, JulieK2. 8–9 – Luoxi. 10–11 – Bowonpat Sakaew, Maridav. 12–13 – MartiBstock, hena cher, Scisetti Alfio, GreenThumbShots, Lees Lens, Verediana Hille. 14–15 – eloresnorwood, myboys.me. 16–17 – MargJohnsonVA, Anna Mente. 18–19 – Creative by Nature, Boyloso, DimaBerlin. 20–21 – Linda Bestwick, Wirestock Creators. 22–23 – fizkes, NikiON.

CONTENTS

Words that look like this can be found in the glossary on page 24.

GROWING SUCCULENTS

Have you ever wondered what makes some plants better than others at surviving in harsh <u>conditions</u>? How do succulents handle hot, dry, desert weather? It has to do with how these plants store water.

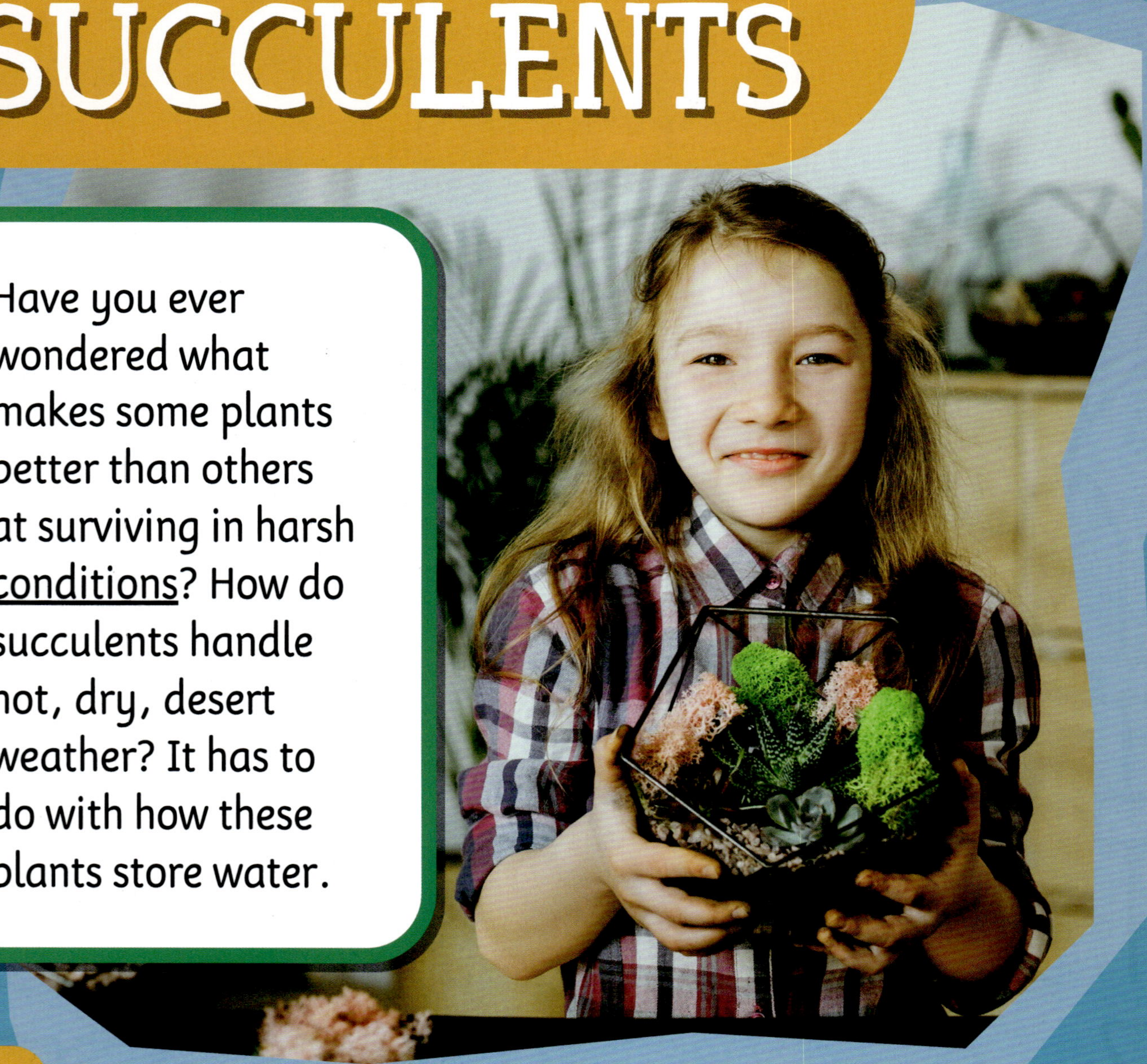

GET YOUR GARDENING GLOVES ON, AND LET'S GET GROWING!

Succulents store water in their stems, leaves, and roots. This gives them a thick, swollen look. Many succulents have a waxy outer layer that keeps water in. These features make them cool plants to grow.

TAKING CUTTINGS

Many plants grow from seeds, including succulents. However, many succulents also <u>reproduce</u> a different way. If certain parts of a succulent break off, new succulents can grow from them. These new, young succulents are called pups.

To get started growing succulents, you can collect a few pieces from a fully grown plant. These pieces are called cuttings. You can twist off a few leaves or cut off the top part of the stem.

DRYING THE CUTTINGS

Most seeds need water as soon as they are planted. However, succulent cuttings must be left to dry before planting. If cuttings are planted while the ends are still wet, they can start to rot.

Drying the ends of cuttings is known as callusing. Put your cuttings in a safe, dry place while they callus over. It may take up to a week.

PREPARING THE SOIL

While you wait for the cuttings to dry, prepare the soil or potting mix you will plant them in. Choose soil that drains easily and dries quickly. Slightly sandy or stony soil is best.

Add the soil to little pots or trays with holes at the bottom. When you water your succulents, any water they do not need will drain through the soil and out of the holes.

PLANTING THE CUTTINGS

Cuttings are like a smaller version of their parent plant. The only thing missing is the roots. Once the cuttings have callused, they can start to grow roots and new leaves.

Some succulent cuttings can be placed on top of the soil. This is usually how leaf cuttings are planted.

Some cuttings should be planted in the soil. This is usually how stem cuttings are planted.

WATERING THE PUPS

You should not water your cuttings until you see that they have grown roots. While they are getting started, the new pups will use the water that is stored inside the parent cuttings.

Once roots have grown, you need to start watering the pups regularly. Only give the plants as much water as they need. Let the soil dry out between waterings.

Too much water can make the roots rot.

REPLANTING THE PUPS

After a while, the parent cuttings will wither as the water in them is used up. That is a sign that your pups are ready to move to a larger space.

Replanting the pups gives them enough room to spread out their roots and grow. As they grow, the pups will take in more sunlight and become bigger plants.

Be careful when replanting. Some succulents have spiky spines.

PROTECTING THE SUCCULENTS

THIS SUCCULENT HAS WITHERED FROM UNDERWATERING.

THIS SUCCULENT HAS BEGUN TO ROT FROM OVERWATERING.

Succulents are not very needy plants, but it is still important to check on them regularly. Underwatering and overwatering can both affect a succulent's health.

Succulents are well suited to being out in the sunlight all day. If you keep your succulents indoors, they need plenty of light. Succulents usually need about 4 to 6 hours of sunlight every day.

FLOWERING

It may take a few years for your succulents to start flowering. While they are young, succulents put most of their energy into growing bigger. They need time to mature enough to bloom.

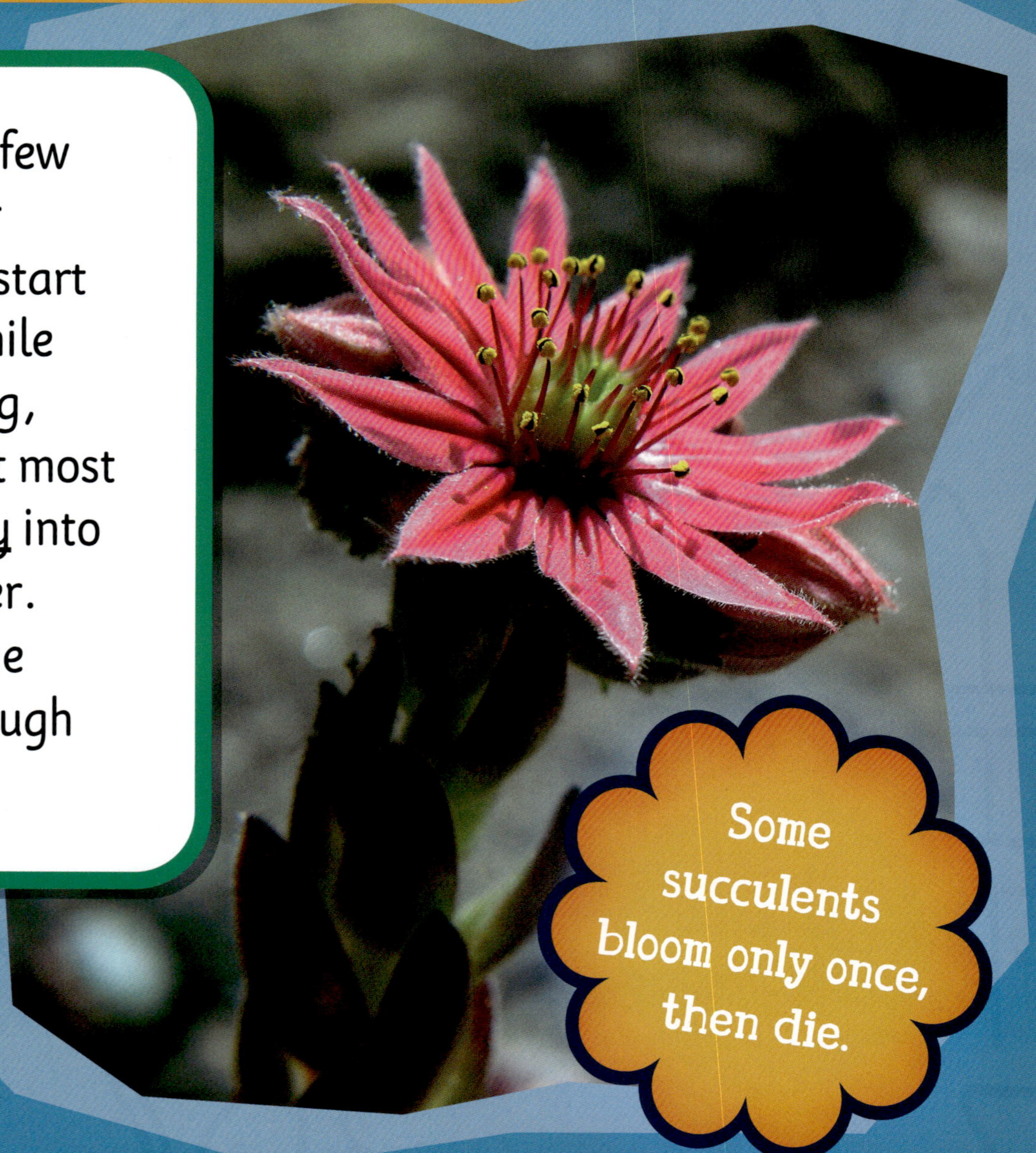

Some succulents bloom only once, then die.

Flowers are how plants make seeds. For seeds to grow, the flowers need to be pollinated. This is when a powder called pollen is moved onto a different plant or a different part of the same plant.

INSECTS PLAY A BIG PART IN POLLINATION.

WHAT WILL YOU GROW?

If you want to try taking care of a plant, succulents are good plants to start with. With a little bit of care and attention, you can grow some really interesting plants.

What kind of succulent would you like to grow? Would you want a spiky cactus? A succulent that flowers every year? A succulent with interesting leaf shapes? There are so many amazing options!

GLOSSARY

CONDITIONS the state of the environment, such as the temperature, rainfall, and food available

DRAINS lets water pour away

ENERGY the power that makes living things able to move and live

MATURE to be fully grown and developed

NEEDY requiring lots of time or attention

POTTING MIX a soil-like planting mixture that water passes through easily

REGULARLY consistently

REPRODUCE to make more of the same thing

STEMS the supporting parts of plants from which leaves often grow

WITHER to shrink and shrivel from lack of water

INDEX